The LAST STRAW

To Eric, Kelly, Randi, and Mike—still feisty after all these years
—PPM

To my dear children
—CPH

Published by Covenant Communications, Inc.
American Fork, Utah

Text Copyright © 2013 by Paula Palangi McDonald
Illustrations Copyright © 2013 Carol Pettit Harding

Printed in China
First Printing: October 2013

19 18 17 16 15 14 13   10 9 8 7 6 5 4 3 2 1

ISBN-13: 978-1-62108-559-1

The Last Straw

WRITTEN BY
PAULA PALANGI MCDONALD

ILLUSTRATED BY
CAROL PETTIT HARDING

Covenant Communications, Inc.

imme that. It's mine!"

"Is not, fatso! I had it first!"

Mom sighed. It was another long, winter afternoon with everyone stuck in the house, and the four little McDonalds were at it again—bickering, teasing, and fighting over their toys. Lately the lively little bunch had been particularly horrible to each other, especially Eric and Kelly, who were just a year apart. The two of them, in particular, seemed determined to spend the whole winter making each other miserable.

With Christmas less than a month away, the McDonald house seemed sadly lacking in Christmas spirit. This was supposed to be the season of sharing and love, of warm feelings and happy hearts. But where were those warm feelings and happy hearts? A home needed more than just pretty packages or twinkling lights on the tree to fill it with the Christmas spirit. How could a mother convince her children that being kind to each other was the most important way to get ready for Christmas?

*M*om had only one idea. She gathered her four little rascals together and sat them down on the stairs, smallest to tallest—Mike, Randi, Kelly, and Eric.

"How would you kids like to start a new Christmas project this year?" she asked. "It's like a game, but it can only be played by people who can keep a secret. Can everyone here do that?"

"I can!" shouted Eric, wildly waving his arm in the air.

"I can keep a secret better than he can," yelled Kelly, jumping up and waving her arms in the air too.

"I can do it!" chimed in Randi. She wasn't quite sure what was happening, but she knew she didn't want to be left out.

"Me too, me too, me too," squealed little Mike, bouncing up and down.

DAD

MOM

ERIC

RANDI

KELLY

MIKE

onderful!" exclaimed Mom. "Here's how the game works. This year we're going to surprise Baby Jesus when He comes on Christmas Eve by making Him the softest bed in the world. We're going to build a little crib for Him to sleep in right here in our house and fill it with straw to make it comfortable. The straw we put in the manger will measure all the kind things we do between now and Christmas. But here's the secret part: we can't let anyone see us doing the good deeds."

"But who will we do the kind things for?" asked Eric.

"We'll do them for each other," Mom explained. "Each week between now and Christmas, we'll put all of our names in this hat—mine and Daddy's too. Then we'll each draw a name and for a whole week we'll do kind things for that person. But here's the hard part: we can't tell anyone whose name we draw."

"Like being a spy!" squealed Randi. "I can do that! I'm a good spy."

om smiled. "Each week we'll try to do as many favors for our special person as we can without getting caught. And for every secret good thing we do, we'll put another straw in the crib. Then on Christmas Eve we'll put Baby Jesus in His little bed, and He'll sleep that night on a bed made of love. I think He'd like that, don't you?"

The children all nodded.

"Now, who will build a little crib for us?" Mom asked.

Eric was the oldest and the only one allowed to use the tools, so he marched off to the basement. There were banging noises and sawing noises, and for a long time there were no noises at all. But finally, Eric climbed back up the stairs with a proud smile. "The best crib in the world!" he grinned. "And I did it all myself."

For once, everyone agreed. The little manger was the best crib in the world, even though one leg was an inch too short and the crib rocked a bit. But it had been built with love—and about a hundred bent nails—so it would certainly last a long time.

"Now we need straw," said Mom, and together they tumbled out to the car to go looking for some.

*S*urprisingly, no one fought over who sat next to the windows that day as they drove around searching for a grassy field. At last they spotted a small, empty lot that had been covered with tall grass in the summer. Now the dried, yellow stalks looked just like real straw.

Mom stopped the car, and, even though it was a bitter cold day, the kids scrambled out to pick handfuls of the tall grass.

"That's enough!" Mom finally laughed when the cardboard box in the trunk was almost overflowing. "Remember, it's only a small crib." So home they went to spread their straw carefully on a tray Mom had put on the kitchen table. The empty manger was placed gently on top, and no one could even notice that it had one short leg.

"When can we pick names? When can we pick?" shouted the children, their faces still rosy from the cold.

"As soon as Daddy comes back from Grandpa's house," Mom answered.

At the supper table that night, the six names were written on separate pieces of paper, folded, and tossed around in an old baseball hat. Then the drawing began.

Kelly picked first and immediately started to giggle. Randi reached into the hat next, trying hard to look like a serious spy. Daddy glanced at his scrap of paper and smiled quietly behind his hand. Mom picked out a name, but her face never gave away a clue. Next, little Mike reached into the hat, but since he couldn't read yet, Daddy had to whisper the name in his ear. Mike then quickly ate his little scrap of paper so no one would ever find out who his secret person was. Eric was the last to choose, and as he unfolded his piece of paper a frown crossed his face. But he stuffed the name into his pocket and said nothing. The family was ready to begin.

The next week was filled with surprises. It seemed the McDonald house had suddenly been invaded by an army of invisible elves, and good things were happening everywhere. Kelly would walk into her room at bedtime and find her little blue nightgown neatly laid out and her bed turned down. Someone cleaned up the sawdust under Daddy's workbench without being asked. The jelly blobs magically disappeared from the kitchen counter after lunch one day while Mom was getting the mail. And every morning, while Eric was brushing his teeth, someone crept quietly into his room and made his bed. It wasn't made perfectly, but it was made. That particular little elf must have had very short arms because he couldn't seem to reach all the way to the middle.

"Where are my shoes?" asked Daddy one morning. No one seemed to know, but before he left for work, they were back in the closet, all shined up.

Mom noticed other changes that week, too. The children weren't teasing or fighting as much. Even Eric and Kelly seemed to be getting along better. In fact, every now and then each of the children could be seen giggling and smiling secret smiles. And slowly, one by one, pieces of straw began to appear in the little crib. At first there were just a few, but then a few more appeared each day. By the end of the first week, there was actually a little pile in the crib. Now, mind you, no one ever saw the straws go in, but later the children could be seen patting and testing the tiny pile for softness.

By Sunday, everyone was anxious to pick new names again, and this time there was more laughter and merriment during the picking process than there had been the first time, except for Eric. Once again he unfolded his slip of paper, looked at it, and stuffed it in his pocket without a word. Mom noticed, as moms always do, but said nothing.

The second week brought more amazing events, and the little pile of straw grew higher and softer. Everyone seemed to be watching and checking it carefully each day. With only two weeks left until Christmas, the children wondered if their homemade bed would be comfortable enough for Baby Jesus.

There is one more thing we need to do to be ready for Christmas Eve," Mom announced on the third Sunday night after they had all picked new names. "We need to find a Baby Jesus for our manger. What can we use?"

"Maybe we can use one of the toys," suggested Randi.

The children ran off to gather up their favorite dolls and stuffed animals. When they had them all lined up on the couch, only an old baby doll, which had been loved almost to pieces, looked like a possibility for their Baby Jesus. Wisps of blonde hair stuck out all over her head, making her look a little lost and forlorn. But her eyes were still bright blue and she still smiled, even though her face was slightly smudged from the touch of so many chubby little fingers.

"I think she's perfect," said Mom. "When Baby Jesus was born He probably didn't have much hair either, and I'll bet He'd like to be represented by a doll who'd had so many hugs."

So it was decided, and the children began to make a new outfit for their Baby Jesus—a little leather vest out of scraps and a diaper out of a dishtowel, because none of them really knew what swaddling clothes were supposed to look like. But Baby Jesus looked just fine in His new clothes, and, best of all, He fit perfectly into the little crib.

Since it wasn't quite Christmas yet, the doll was laid carefully on a shelf in the hall closet to wait for Christmas Eve and a softer bed.

eanwhile, the pile of straw grew and grew. Every day brought new and different surprises as the secret elves stepped up their activity. There was more laughter, less teasing, and hardly any meanness around the house. The McDonald home was finally filled with Christmas spirit. Only Eric was unusually quiet, and sometimes Mom would catch him looking a little sad and unhappy. But the straw in the manger continued to pile up.

At last it was almost Christmas. The final Sunday night of name picking was the night before Christmas Eve. As the family sat around the table Mom said, "You've all done a wonderful job. There must be hundreds of straws in our manger—maybe a thousand. You should be so pleased with the bed you've made. But remember, there's still one whole day left. We all have time to do a little more to make the bed even softer before tomorrow night. Let's do our best."

The children smiled as they looked at their fluffy pile of straw. No one needed to test it anymore. They all knew it was comfortable and soft. But maybe they could still make it a little deeper, a little softer. They were going to try.

For the last time, the hat was passed around the table. Little Mike picked out a name, Daddy whispered it to him, then Mike quickly ate the paper just as he had done every week. Randi unfolded hers carefully under the table, peeked at it, and then hunched up her little shoulders, smiling. Kelly reached into the hat and giggled happily when she saw the name. Mom and Daddy each took their turns too, and then Daddy handed the hat with the last name to Eric. But as Eric unfolded the small scrap of paper and read it, his face pinched up and without a word, he stood and ran from the room.

Everyone jumped up from the table, but Mom stopped them. "No! Stay where you are," she said. "Let me talk to him alone first."

Just as she reached the top of the stairs, Eric's door banged open. He had a small suitcase in one hand and was trying to pull his coat on with the other.

"I have to leave," he mumbled quietly through his tears. "If I don't, I'll spoil Christmas for everyone."

"But why? And where are you going?" asked Mom.

"I can sleep in my snow fort for a couple of days. I'll come home right after Christmas, I promise."

om started to say something about freezing and snow and no mittens or boots, but Daddy, who was now standing just behind her, put his hand on her arm and shook his head. The front door closed, and together they watched from the window as the little figure with the sadly slumped shoulders and no hat trudged across the street and sat down on a snowbank near the corner. It was very dark outside, and cold, and a few snow flurries drifted down on the small boy and his suitcase.

"But he'll freeze!" said Mom.

"Give him a few minutes alone," Daddy said quietly. "Then go talk to him."

The huddled figure was already dusted with white ten minutes later when Mom walked across the street and sat down beside him on the snowbank.

"What is it, Eric? You've been so good these last weeks, but I know something's been bothering you since we first started the manger. Can you tell me, honey?"

"Aw, Mom, don't you see?" he sniffled. "I tried so hard, but I can't do it anymore, and now I'm going to wreck Christmas for everyone." With that he burst into sobs and threw himself into Mom's arms.

"But I don't understand," Mom said, brushing the tears from his face. "What can't you do? And how could you possibly spoil Christmas for us?"

For that very reason, just before bedtime, Mom tiptoed quietly to Kelly's room to lay out the little blue nightgown and turn down the bed. But she stopped in the doorway, surprised. Someone had already been there. The nightgown was laid neatly across the bed, and a small red race car rested next to it on the pillow.

The last straw was Eric's after all.

The next day the whole family was busy cooking and straightening up the house for Christmas Day, wrapping last-minute presents, and trying hard to keep from bursting with excitement. But even with all the activity and eagerness, a flurry of new straws piled up in the manger, and by nightfall it was almost overflowing. At different times, while passing by, each member of the family, big and small, would pause and look at the wonderful pile for a moment, then smile before going on. At last, it was almost time for the tiny crib to be used. But . . . who could really know? One straw might still make a difference.

M om," the little boy choked, "you just don't know. I got Kelly's name *all four times!* I can't do one more nice thing for her or I'll die! I tried, Mom. I really did. I snuck into her room every night and fixed her bed. I even laid out her crummy nightgown. And one day I let her use my race car, but she smashed it right into the wall like always!

"I tried to be nice to her, Mom. Even when she saw that the crib leg was too short and called me a dummy for it later, I didn't hit her. And every week, when we picked new names I thought it would be over. But tonight, when I got her name again, I knew I couldn't do one more nice thing for her. Mom, I just can't! If I try, I'll probably punch her instead. And tomorrow's Christmas Eve. If I beat up Kelly, I'll spoil Christmas for everybody just when we're ready to put Baby Jesus in the crib. Don't you see why I had to leave?"

They sat together quietly for a few minutes, Mom's arm around Eric's shoulders. Finally, Mom spoke softly. "Eric, I'm so proud of you. Every good thing you did should count double because it was especially hard for you to be nice to Kelly for so long. You gave your love when it wasn't easy to give. Maybe that's what the spirit of Christmas is really all about.

"You're the one who's probably added the most important straws to the crib, and you can be proud of yourself. Now, how would you like a chance to earn a few easy straws like the rest of us? I still have the name I picked tonight in my pocket, and I haven't looked at it yet. Why don't we switch, just for the last day? It will be our secret."

"That's not cheating?"

"It's not cheating." Mom smiled, and she took the slip of paper from her pocket and handed it to him.

Together they dried the tears, brushed off the snow, and walked back to the house.